Successful
Event
Management

in a week

BRIAN SALTER
& NAOMI LANGFORD-WOOD

Hodder & Stoughton

A MEMBER OF THE HODDER HEADLINE GROUP

Orders: please contact Bookpoint Ltd, 39 Milton Park, Abingdon, Oxon OX14 4TD.
Telephone: (44) 01235 400414, Fax: (44) 01235 400454. Lines are open from 9.00 -
6.00, Monday to Saturday, with a 24 hour message answering service.
Email address: orders@bookpoint.co.uk

British Library Cataloguing in Publication Data
A catalogue record for this title is available from The British Library

ISBN 0 340 757809

First published 1999
Impression number   10 9 8 7 6 5 4 3 2 1
Year   2005 2004 2003 2002 2001 2000 1999

Typeset by Multiplex Techniques Ltd, St Mary Cray, Kent.
Printed in Great Britain for Hodder & Stoughton Educational, a division of
Hodder Headline Plc, 338 Euston Road, London NW1 3BH by Cox & Wyman Ltd,
Reading, Berkshire.

the Institute of Management

FOUNDATION

The mission of the Institute of Management (IM) is to promote the art and science of management.

The Institute embraces all levels of management from student to chief executive and supports its own Foundation which provides a unique portfolio of services for all managers, enabling them to develop skills and achieve management excellence.

For information on the various levels and benefits of membership, please contact:

Department HS
Institute of Management,
Cottingham Road,
Corby,
Northants NN17 1TT.
Tel: 01536 204222
Fax: 01536 201651.

This series is commissioned by the Institute of Management Foundation.

C O N T E N T S

Every business gets involved with events in one way or another, whether it is a major corporate exhibition or something put on at the village hall to promote a local product or interest group. Most of us have at some time or another attended exhibitions, conferences, seminars or other such events, but there is a world of difference between being a mere participant on the one hand, and having to shoulder the responsibility for staging it in the first place.

Events come in all shapes and sizes, from trade exhibitions to focused seminars and conferences, and they all need clear objectives to be identified so that the right mix of skills can ensure success – once you've got the vision right.

Managing events successfully requires:

- clear objectives
- an appropriate and interesting concept
- meticulous planning
- more marketing than you thought was necessary
- lateral vision
- a great deal of stamina
- good teamwork
- a realistic post mortem – for better planning next time.

Sometimes events can be like wartime situations or a game of Monopoly as they tend to bring out the best and worst in people. You can achieve a successful event with a modest budget if you have a good concept and employ meticulous planning with a good team of people.

Whether you've managed an event of any sort before or not, *Successful Event Management in a Week* aims to help you iron out the wrinkles in the planning stages so that the execution is as pain free as possible, making the overall event not only a success but even something to be enjoyed.

Over the next week we will be looking at:

- the different types of event suitable for a business to consider
- the planning, preparation and logistics of staging an event
- the people you need to ensure your event is a success
- some of the essentials many would rather forget – such as the legal and financial implications
- publicity and marketing your event
- getting through the big day itself
- clearing up and holding the post mortem, for there are always lessons to be learned for the next time!

If there is one piece of advice that we would offer up this early in the book, it is this. There are many different ways to manage your event. It is a truism that it tends not to matter what decision you make as long as you make it early enough in the planning stages, stick to it and make sure that everyone you are working with knows what that decision is.

Putting on a successful event can at times be fraught as you rush around getting everything done by 'yesterday'; but there is little to compare with the satisfaction of knowing that an event that you have organised has been a tremendous success.

Focus on the objectives

In all the years we have been organising events it has never ceased to surprise us how many people set off vainly attempting to organise something without having the faintest idea of what they actually hope to achieve, nor of allowing enough time to do it in.

Many of these events have turned out to be highly successful, but as often as not that happens by chance rather than by design. It is all too common for company management not to appreciate the time and effort needed to organise a successful event, and it is almost routine to find exhibitors (and event managers) who leave everything to the last minute and then expect everyone else to drop whatever they are doing simply to rescue them from the sticky mess they have got themselves into.

Things can go horribly wrong from day one if:

- the basic objectives of an event are not identified
- insufficient time is allowed to arrange the event
- the marketing is not realistically planned
- the person in overall charge lacks the necessary experience.

Above all a successful organiser should have the ability to think laterally and to pull together a disparate series of events. If he has a sense of the theatrical, too, then all well and good. Any event, be it a conference, exhibition or seminar, can be thought of as industrial theatre as it will use many of the techniques to be found on the stage. An understanding of these will often, therefore, be of considerable help.

Another necessary attribute of a successful organiser is the ability to think logically, quickly and clearly, especially at times of great pressure. Panic can all too easily set in when others begin to appreciate fast approaching deadlines; and a cool head with an active brain is a wonderful asset to possess at this time.

Perhaps more than anything else, though, an organiser will find his task less of an ordeal if he is able to keep both a sense of perspective, as well as a sense of humour. The staging of an event will often bring out some of the following:

1. Euphoria for having been given the task
2. Confusion over what exactly it is that the person commissioning the event wants to achieve
3. Disenchantment with all those no-hoper hangers-on
4. The search to root out the guilty
5. Punishment of the innocent
6. Distinction for those who contributed least

Cynical? Never! Just ask any events manager and the chances are that most, if not all, will recognise this sequence all too well. However, with human nature as it is, sufficient time needs to be allocated to reassure your team about the part they will play in achieving success for the forthcoming event.

Defining the objectives

So having got over the initial euphoria, let's just sit down a moment and define what it is we are hoping to achieve by staging this event. Only once we have defined our objectives will we be able to make the correct decision as to the type of event that will be most appropriate.

- Is the objective to impart information, or to act as an incentive?
- Will you be launching a product, rewarding the great and the good, or encouraging others to do better?
- Who will be your audience? Will it be held purely within the confines of your organisation, or will it be open to the world at large?

If you don't know the answers to these most basic questions, then how can you hope to know at the end of the event if you have been successful or not?

In setting objectives it is useful to consider:

1. What do I want to achieve?
2. With whom do I wish to communicate?
3. When should I do so?
4. Where should this take place?
5. Why do I want to do it in the first place?
6. How will I communicate this?

Be quite clear. It is all too easy for someone to decide first on the content, and then to let the content determine the objective. We have seen it happen on countless occasions; but that really is a case of putting the cart before the horse. If we appear to be stressing the obvious, then please bear with us. It is of such fundamental importance that we find it truly staggering how many people potentially throw away goodwill, money and opportunity, all for the lack of a little thought.

What's in a name?

Up until this point we have had to be careful in our use of the word 'event'. There are many different types of event in which any organisation might be interested. Principally these will include:

- Exhibitions
- Conferences
- Seminars
- Meetings
- Award ceremonies
- Gala dinners
- Corporate hospitality

Exhibitions

Every year in Britain nearly 100,000 stands are constructed at exhibitions up and down the country. Exhibitions and trade fairs should be regarded as a major part of the marketing process. Although they have changed in many different ways since the original trade fairs in France of two centuries ago, the basic idea has remained the same. In essence, they provide the ideal environment in which people of like minds or shared interests can come together in order to do business.

Exhibitions fall into three basic categories:

1. Trade and industrial fairs
2. Consumer/public events
3. Single company events

It is hardly surprising that with the plethora of vertical markets, where manufacturers and service providers wish to communicate with potential customers, that there are very many more trade shows than public exhibitions. Indeed, organisers of exhibitions and trade bodies take great care to avoid clashing dates with other shows within that market sector around the world. Many exhibitions are planned at least a year in advance, and sometimes as much as two years, since there are, relatively speaking, only a limited number of venues that exhibition organisers wish to book.

One of the principal reasons for exhibiting is that it provides an ideal vehicle to meet potential clients. Both parties – buyer and seller – can get to know one another, but it also provides an ideal opportunity to size up the opposition. In fact, you can usually gain a very clear picture of your competitors since many people out of their home environment are inclined to give out too much information when they might do better to keep their powder dry.

With the trend for tighter niche marketing, it is now becoming the norm for trade exhibitions to be tightly focused. Nowhere is this more so than in the computer market where the general computer shows of the 80s and early 90s have now given way to specialist shows on the Internet, networking or multimedia, for instance.

As competition amongst show organisers increases, so has the level of customer service expected by both the exhibitors and delegates. It has now become commonplace for the larger exhibitions to offer their exhibitors some form of electronic processing to ease the task of evaluating and following up potential leads. Visitors, too, are being better looked after with improved pre-show information and fast-track entry to the show.

As well as this, it is also becoming increasingly common to find parallel events being staged in close proximity to the exhibition itself. There may be seminars or working demonstrations that go hand in hand with the theme of the show and are more likely, therefore, to attract audiences.

A word of caution, however. Not only should the exhibition and parallel events be held in the same building – or extremely close to it, at least – but care should be taken to ensure that the delegates have enough time to visit the stands as well as sit in on the talks or demonstrations, otherwise the overall event will have failed through simply not being able to satisfy expectations.

Having made up your mind to exhibit, then, you should recap on your objectives:

- the introduction of new products or services to the marketplace
- the demonstration of existing products or services
- test marketing products or services
- raising the profile of your product
- brand awareness
- reinforcing relationships with customers
- entering new export markets
- supporting your trade association

At the end of the day, though, the bottom line is that you as an organisation should be able to sell your goods and services more profitably and to increase your market share.

Conferences

In business it is often necessary to attempt to change the way people think. A well planned and executed conference can enthuse a sales force, persuade employees to change their working practices or launch a new or unfamiliar product to a specialist audience. Above all, it can enable people to come together and communicate with one another more effectively.

Just as with the term 'exhibition', a conference can be hard to define exactly. There *are* many different types of conference, but they all have one thing in common: they aim to convey a particular idea to an audience.

The Sales Conference

Sales people are vital to the success of many businesses, and the Sales Conference can offer a unique opportunity to meet and talk to them all. Sales people can also be some of the toughest audiences in the world; they are more likely to know the true worth of your products since it is they who are at the sharp end of your business. Equally, being out on the road can be a lonely job and the sales conference can be an ideal opportunity to prove to them that they are valued members of your team.

Corporate roadshows

A roadshow can prove to be an ideal vehicle where your intended audience is spread apart geographically. A large corporate, for instance, might have branches across the country and it would be impracticable to bring all the staff together under one roof and at one time.

The effectiveness of a series of roadshows often comes down to a most basic point of planning. If you try to stage an event which was a success in a large venue, such as a conference hall or spacious exhibition venue, then it will be courting disaster to try to recreate it in miniature. But if you know the likely venues early on in the planning stages, then it is usually pretty straightforward to plan the events in tandem.

If you are planning to take your roadshow to a good number of locations, rather than two or three, then it is usually a good idea to consult the professionals. Putting on one show can be a lot of work to get it right; organising many together can be a logistical and practical nightmare unless suitably qualified people are in place from inception.

The AGM

Planning an annual general meeting for a company can prove to be a huge undertaking, and not something for the feint-hearted. On the one hand you might get well over 1,000 people turning up; on the other hand there might only be a handful. One AGM we were once involved in was held on the day of an important World Cup match. A large hall was booked for the expected audience, but in the event, directors outnumbered the shareholders by three to one!

Shareholder audiences can reflect a large cross section of the general public. There may be financially savvy fund managers, together with many small investors. Both will want reassurance that their investments are being looked after wisely. In such a situation, therefore, it is important to appreciate that any elaborate state-of-the-art gizmos and technical wizardry designed to impress, are more likely to get your audience wondering if their hard-earned investment money could be put to better use elsewhere.

...and other conferences

There are plenty of other types of conference: press conferences, financial presentations, product launches and, increasingly common, video conferences all come immediately to mind. However, just as with the AGM, it is vital to work out the objective of your conference and the best method to achieve that objective, if it is to be a success.

Seminars and Meetings
We've lumped these two categories together since in many ways they have so much in common. The objective that anyone has in staging such an event is to exchange information. Here it is the role of the organiser not to create the presentation, but rather to create the right conditions for others to be able to do so successfully.

Because their success is so dependent on the basics that you provide, it is vital that you leave nothing to chance. Far too many conference venues promise the earth when it comes to providing simple audio-visual equipment, but unless you have tried and tested it don't be surprised on the big day if it lets you down.

With the increasing use of computers in presentations, this is particularly true of the plethora of projectors offered up to the hapless organiser. They are not cheap to buy, can be expensive to hire, and are prone to going wrong at the last minute or being incompatible with older PCs. Some computer projections can only be seen in a darkened room which may not be at all what your presenters had in mind. So check, check, check, if you want to sleep comfortably the night before.

Corporate hospitality

Many people don't make the connection between event management and corporate hospitality. Yet if you think about it, meticulous planning is clearly necessary to ensure a successful outcome. Why would you want to lay on corporate hospitality if it were not to impress the hell out of your potential, or existing, clients – or engender a comfort zone which makes them more likely to come to you for business – anyway?

Under this umbrella we can also include:

- Gala dinners
- Award ceremonies
- Activity days - such as golf, motor racing, fashion and makeovers, war-games and general team building – for both personal development and hospitality.

All of these activities need to be planned in the same manner as conferences and exhibitions, and suitable check lists need to be created so that nothing is forgotten.

Having decided upon the type of event we wish to put on, there are plenty of other decisions that have to be made. Tomorrow we shall start by considering venues and working out a proper planning process. But as long as we have properly worked out our objectives and thought through the theme and content, then we're well on the way to getting this show on the road!

Planning and preparation

Of the many important decisions that an event organiser
has to make, the choice of venue, timing of the event and
its structure are keys to success. The choice of venue can
make or break the smooth running and success of any 'do',
be it a conference, exhibition or seminar. Sometimes the
very nature of the event will dictate this decision. Perhaps
it has always been held in a specific location, or if it is an
exhibition the chances are that you will have little or no say
in the matter.

Unfortunately it is one of those facts of life that very many
venues are really quite unsuitable for the type of event they
are aiming to house. Remember that first impressions really
do count, especially when you are trying to impress. If you
are let down by

- the location
- poor catering
- poor service
- inadequate services

then the event can quite literally be ruined. There are
numerous stories of conferences, especially, which have
turned out to be absolute disasters simply because a few
simple ground rules and attention to detail had been left to
chance.

So how do you ensure that a venue for your event is an
ideal one? The first thing to do, of course, is to ask yourself
some of the following basic questions:

1. How long will the event be?
2. How many delegates are there likely to be attending?
3. How far will they have to travel?
4. What budget is allowed?
5. What are the overall aims of the event?
6. Is distance from the office of greater or lesser importance than the distance that delegates have to travel?
7. Will anyone need overnight accommodation?

The budget

Perhaps the best place to start is by considering your overall expenditure. In a traditional, hierarchically structured company, senior managers may well expect a better quality of venue than their junior colleagues. However, in the looser, flatter-structured companies that are now becoming more the norm, everyone will expect to be treated in the same way. So decide where the overall balance will lie and the effect that any one particular venue is going to have on the cachet of the event.

The location

Having decided the price band, check out the travel times and suitability of various locations. It simply is no good selecting a superb location if there is little public transport, or it is difficult to find, or access is poor.

Sometimes the geographical location is as important as the hotel or conference centre itself. One organisation we worked for recently decided that although its previous annual conference in Manchester had been satisfactory, this year they wanted something a little bit special. They chose the conference centre at Disneyland near Paris. It was easy to get to, had ample accommodation in January which is when they always held their conferences, there were plenty of things for spouses and partners to do and see, and to get the four day event off to a great start, arrangements were made to take all 100 plus delegates to the Moulin Rouge nightclub on the first evening.

As far as accessibility is concerned, Eurodisney – as it was previously called – is 'just down the road' from Paris CDG Airport, it has a TGV station on its doorstep and even has Eurostar trains making not-infrequent visits. The event was a huge success, helped not in small part by the fact that everyone started off in a very positive frame of mind, thanks to the thought given to the logistics.

Of course, it is impossible to lay down firm rules about location. Just as transport and accessibility may be important considerations for some, almost the exact opposite might be required where secrecy and security are involved. Many board meetings or inter-company negotiations are specifically held in remote or secluded hotels so as not to set off jittery City analysts jumping on the back of rumour and counter-rumour.

Sometimes, also, a rural location will be sought after as an antidote for delegates arriving from a town or city or to give a better environment for brainstorming activities. The change in environment can do wonders for preparing people for a totally different work experience.

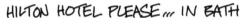

Venue categories

Just as the location is extremely important, so too is the type of venue for your event. Venues fall into six main categories:

1. Purpose-built exhibition centres
2. Purpose-built conference centres
3. Large meeting rooms in hotels
4. College, university and other educational meeting facilities
5. Centres off the beaten track
6. Specific activity centres

Purpose-built centres are often a 'safe' choice because you can usually reckon on the fact that others will have worked out solutions to the problems that any event organiser will face. Catering, in particular, is likely to be tried and tested for the particular number of delegates for whom such venues will have been designed.

Hotels, on the other hand, vary greatly in the facilities on offer, the level of service delegates can expect, the standard of catering and the quality of accommodation. Many hotels recognise the importance that conference and exhibition bookings can play as far as their profits are concerned, and make an all-out effort to entice them in. But technical facilities in many can be quite basic and car parking can also be limited.

Colleges and universities are under growing pressure to boost revenues and in vacation times, especially, can offer highly competitive rates. Purpose-built lecture halls can be advantageous, especially for the staging of seminars and training sessions. However, sometimes the overall level of accommodation and catering can leave something to be desired, although some contract professional caterers to entice more business.

While a centre off the beaten track may fulfil some of the functions you need for a particular kind of meeting, you have to weigh up these with the possible problems of transport and communications that we often take for granted. If the delegates are high-powered enough to need to hide away for a meeting, then the chances are that they will also need excellent communications links and those end-of-the-day home comforts. Some hideaways – especially country hotels – provide total luxury and cater for this type of occasion as their main source of business.

Activity centres are often thought to be the ideal venues for team-building events, though many tend to be a bit rugged and might leave something to be desired in the way of home comforts. Mountaineering, paintball fighting, go-kart racing, shooting, and so on are typical activities that identify characteristics and help in defining roles and building teams. Nevertheless, these centres recognise the importance of catering for business events and have tailored their products accordingly to great effect. Many provide all the kit needed so that the delegates only need to provide for their everyday requirements.

The site visit

Once your list of possible venues has been whittled down it is absolutely essential for the organiser to pay a visit to each, preferably incognito and also when another meeting is going on. That might not always be possible, but under such conditions you are much more likely to be able to weigh up the look and feel of the place and judge its suitability. Inspections are important because you can never tell from a brochure or web site what the downsides of any venue are.

Experienced organisers often make a point of travelling to the potential venue in the same way that most delegates will and record their first impressions onto dictation recorders as they walk around. Some even carry Polaroid cameras, digital cameras or camcorders for easy recall of certain rooms or areas later on, and this is especially a good idea when a large number of rooms are being inspected.

They say that first impressions make lasting impressions, and you should always therefore check out the following:

- the attitude of the staff
- the quality of accommodation
- the style, colour and condition of the furnishings
- the formality of the venue or room
- the ease of moving from one area to another – such as from the room or hall to the coffee area
- the adequacy of the room's ventilation
- the availability of ante-rooms or small meeting rooms if delegates need to split up into small groups
- the rules regarding the positioning of banners and posters
- whether the venue will be shared with other organisations
- the provision of telephones.

We all know of meetings that have been set up at short notice, and as a result it has been necessary for the organiser to accept whatever he can find, regardless of its suitability. But this can be costly, both in financial terms as well as in terms of whether the venue will have served the purpose of the event. Remember, a badly planned event is often worse than no event at all.

As a guide, it can usually take between one and two hours to fully check out a venue. Ask to speak to the person responsible for handling corporate events. Normally this will be the banqueting or conference executive, but their titles can vary widely. Don't put up with just speaking to the sales manager. He won't be looking after you on the actual day – if you get as far as making a booking. You need to know exactly what you can expect to get, and you should not hold back on any questions for fear of offending anyone.

As a rule of thumb, one good way of telling how well a hotel is run is to ask to see some of the rooms that your delegates will *not* be using. This way you can see what has been prepared specifically for your appointed inspection. You could even ask to see the kitchens. Good food is essential for any event and is too often relegated to a lesser importance on purely a cost factor. So, look for tell-tale signs of grease on the floors and check out the kitchen staff.

In general, if their uniforms are clean and they look happy the chances are that the hotel is well run; and, if nothing else, ask for references.

If the room is to be laid out for a conference, then do you have a choice in the way the chairs are positioned? On numerous occasions we have experienced what has at first seemed like an ideal room, only to find that because of a support pillar or some other obstruction, floor space has had to be sacrificed. Low ceilings are another no-no as far as successful venues are concerned. When delegates have to spend long hours in that one location, it can become extremely claustrophobic and oppressive after a very short time.

The formality or informality of the layout of the furniture will play a major role in how much space you should allow for each delegate. Seating can be laid out in a variety of styles – theatre style, classroom style, boardroom style, around round tables, square tables, oblong tables – and this can range from allowing about 1 m^2 per delegate for a reception to perhaps 4 m^2 in a meeting, depending on table layout. Back projection of slides, AV or films can also take up valuable space. Normally, however, the venue executive can advise on this. The space will also work better if you do not overfill it. Remember, though, that if you are given a maximum number of delegates for a particular room, you should not go above that. Fire regulations together with other specifications laid down by the Health and Safety Executive are not open for discussion and must be adhered to at all times.

Lighting is another factor that affects delegates, and some

of the worst venues for conferences and other meetings especially have no natural daylight whatsoever. Although a large picture window can be very distracting if you are trying to hold the attention of your delegates, the feeling of claustrophobia in a totally artificially-lit room is many times worse, and we would advise that you should make a point of rejecting such a room out of hand.

Intrusive noise should of course be avoided at all costs. Often it is only on the day itself that such a nuisance rears its ugly head, but you can still look out for any tell-tale signs, such as close proximity to kitchens, lifts, outside walls overlooking a car park or motorway, and squeaky floors and doors.

Timing

In a book that purports to deal with events of any kind, there can be no hard and fast rule about how much preparation time needs to be allowed to make it a success. Setting up everything needed for an exhibition will often take many months of hard work; added to that you also need to consider the lead times for publicity, stand build and ordering of any special items required on the day. Conferences, seminars and other meetings may need less time in physically preparing for the show, but if you are aiming to entice people to your event, then they will need to book their diaries, sometimes months in advance. So leave nothing to the last minute, for down that route lies instant disappointment.

The market sector in which you are operating will often determine the most suitable time of year for the event to be held. The vast majority of events are held in the spring and autumn. In the summer months many people are away on holiday, whilst the winter can prove a difficult time for travel – though this may mean that better rates are negotiable at these times of year. On the other hand, the annual conference in Paris that we referred to earlier was for the horticultural sector, so winter was an ideal time when the delegates normally experience a lull in their sales cycle.

In preparing for an event, some kind of time planner is invaluable. Whereas a piece of graph paper might well have sufficed in the 'old days' it is now quite common for organisers to make use of computer software which prepare Gannt charts, that graphically display time lines and dependencies. One of the best, and most widely used software packages is Microsoft's *Project*.

Task Name	Duration	28 Aug '94							04 Sep '94							11 Sep '94							18 Sep '94							2
		S	S	M	T	W	T	F	S	S	M	T	W	T	F	S	S	M	T	W	T	F	S	S	M	T	W	T	F	S	S	M
Cleanup crew	1d																															
Arrangements	**80h**																															
Transportation	1d																															
Event transport	3d																															
Flowers	4d	0%																														
Table decoration	1d							0%																								
Lighting	1d							0%																								
Event Preparation	**48h**																															
Buy room decoration	1d									0%																						
Buy party favors	1d									0%																						
Setup equipment for ·	2d										0%																					
Decorate	2d												0%																			
Special Event	**0d**														14/09																	
Event Wrap-up	**72h**																															
Cleanup	2d																	0%														
Pay bills	4d																		0%													
Write thank you lett	2d																							0%								
Write event summary	1d																													0%		
Vacation	**0d**																															

A typical Gannt chart as displayed by Microsoft *Project*

The importance of planning

The importance of the planning stages for any event cannot be over-stressed. Exhibitions, especially, require a great deal of co-ordination between different teams of players (we'll be looking at this tomorrow) and without adequate planning the opportunities for confusion, oversight and mistakes are considerable.

Ask the stand managers after an exhibition how successful they thought the event proved for them and it is likely that you will get a variety of answers. Some may well have got very many orders or positive sales leads, whilst others may well ask themselves why they bothered going in the first place. Invariably their responses will be directly proportional to the amount of pre-show planning – or lack of it – as well as, and perhaps more importantly, the aches in their feet and how tired they are!

By planning properly, you will also have a better understanding of whether your event was successful, or not. If you organise everything on an off-the-cuff basis, then how can you go back to check how you might be able to do something better next time around? If you are to fully appraise the effects of the event when you do your post mortem it is essential to put in some pegs of expectations and bench marks by which to measure success – with the wisdom of hindsight.

Remember, too, that by taking part in any public event you are opening up your organisation to public scrutiny. If the stand or venue looks shoddy, then what does that say about your organisation? If your staff are ill-informed or rude, then what confidence will your potential customers have?

But if the stand is smart, and your staff are polite, approachable and knowledgeable then the image of your organisation will be positive for all to see and remember.

Structuring your event

As important as the venue is the structure of your event. Your delegates are, after all, only human, and providing them with hard chairs for a seminar, allowing sessions to go on for too long without leaving time for 'natural' breaks, not providing the necessary back-up information for delegates or ignoring what delegates are able to do in their free time (especially if the event goes into two or more days) is guaranteed to lead to discomfort and even ill feeling. Who was it, after all, who formulated the theory that a person's attention span is inversely proportional to the numbness of his buttocks?

With this in mind, careful attention needs to be given to:

- the timing of seminar sessions
- the content of delegate packs
- the mix of speakers
- the after-event entertainment
- the adequacy of toilet facilities
- the availability of catering
- the adequacy of the technical facilities

We will be looking in more detail tomorrow at the necessity of getting good people on your team, including the use of professionals where appropriate. But today we have focused on the one central message:

There are three essential ingredients for any successful event, be it a conference, seminar, exhibition, or any other type of meeting:

1. Planning
2. Planning
3. *Always* planning

So tomorrow, let's start considering how we can put some of those plans into action.

Choosing your people

As a rough rule of thumb, the physical organisation of a three day conference for 250 people takes an absolute minimum of six working weeks. An exhibition can take considerably longer. But this does not mean that you can mount a *successful* event in six weeks time.

At all kinds of events there are a myriad of things to think about, plan for and action in order that the failure of one little detail does not result in the entire event being considered a flop. So where do you start? Whom are you going to rope in to help with the organisation of what could be a highly prestigious event?

The first decision has to be whether you form an organising committee, with an appointed leader, or go it alone. On the one hand, spreading the load can help in reducing the pressure; on the other hand… well, we all know about too many cooks and their effect on broth.

For a really successful event, there has to be one supremo – someone who makes the final decision on aspects of the event. It's generally true that it really doesn't matter whether the organiser chooses route A or B, as long as he comes down firmly in one camp. There is no place for the ditherer, since not only is time usually of the essence, but a clear signal needs to be sent out to all who are playing their part in getting the show together that someone is in charge.

Good channels of communication are vital to the overall success of the event, especially between the organiser and the technical crews – the people who will look after the lighting, the staging and all the other aspects involved.

In drawing up the team it is vital to be perfectly honest with yourself and ask what specialist tasks there are that are simply outside the scope of the lay organiser. It may well be possible that some of your in-house people can help, and certainly it is worth exploring this avenue, especially if your budget is tight. If your exhibition or meeting is small, it is also possible that you can do it all with the help of in-company people, but the larger the event, the more call on resources there will be.

A safer route may well be to find a professional organiser, but here you should be aware that professional *event* and *conference* organisers and professional *exhibition* organisers have very different roles. On the one hand, a conference organiser's main role is in administration; but an exhibition organiser's main role is to promote the exhibition. If that seems odd to you, then think about it this way.

The point about staging an exhibition is to get a targeted audience physically in front of your products, display or whatever. The exhibition organiser will, of course, handle a great many other things, but most of the time he will subcontract out the work on building your stand, supplying the electrics, organising the printing of your display material, fixing the lighting and so on.

Employing professionals

If you do decide to employ an exhibition organiser, it is essential to get one who has a track record of organising in your own particular market sector. There are plenty of places where you can look for such a person.

- Some are 'owned' by particular venues, but be aware that their priorities and allegiance is to the venue, rather than to you!
- Most trade associations either have them as members, or can recommend some.
- Journals often set up exhibitions as a promotion for their own range of magazines, and again it may be cost effective to use their organisers who are already 'on tap'.
- There are plenty of commercial firms solely involved in organising exhibitions (conferences and other events also have their own specialists) – you can find their advertisements in many magazines and directories, but you can also get a list of members from the *Association of Exhibition Organisers* (26 Chapter Street, London SW1).

Whether you use a professional organiser or not, you will still need to think carefully about the design of your stand,

and for this the services of a professional designer usually proves to be money well spent. Stand and set design, as well as construction, is a complex process which involves graphic design, structural engineering, copywriting and even human psychology. Go to any exhibition and you will see some stands that quite literally draw the visitor in, whilst others have the totally opposite effect. It's not difficult to see which were designed professionally and which were constructed with a tight budget very much in mind!

Unless you plump for a 'shell-scheme' stand (that may well be perfectly satisfactory for a small display-type exhibition: see below), designing in three dimensions, allowing people enough space to move around and, at the same time; creating a visual impact requires considerable skill. Add to that the fact that the stand must be robust – for you obviously do not want it to collapse from the sheer weight of numbers – and it is pretty evident that this is a job for the skilled professional.

When choosing a designer you have a choice of going to an independent advisor or to the event's stand contractor directly. There are arguments for going down either route; it's analogous to the situation where you want to build an extension on your house. You can either find an architect who will design the extension and advise or brief a builder himself, or else you can go directly to a builder on the basis that he should be able to build an extension in a tried and tested fashion.

The independent designer route will usually cost a little more, whereas stand construction companies come in all shapes and sizes. Whilst some work with a particular modular display system, others specialise in custom-built designs. As many stand constructors include a 'free' design consultancy as part of their overall package, in general you get what you pay for.

For those involved with smaller exhibitions, a 'shell-scheme' stand may be all that is required. The shell-scheme will normally be supplied by the contractor working for the exhibition organiser, but you will still need to think about the interior layout along with the graphics and display panels and any working surfaces that will be needed. Again, just as the shell-scheme comes in a modular form, so too can you buy or rent out modular furniture to fill your space.

Drawing up your shortlist

One of the best ways we know of choosing both designers
and contractors is to visit a number of exhibitions and
events to make a note of which stands impress you. Most
exhibitors will be only too pleased to pass on the names of
those responsible. Alternatively you could ask the
organisers whom they would recommend. You should
normally be able to get three or four names in this way.

In drawing up your final shortlist, don't ignore the
following factors:

- Does your designer use a computer aided design
  system? If so, many of the more recent 3D
  packages will allow you to 'walk through' your stand
  in virtual reality, giving you a good feel for what the
  stand will be like once it's built.
- Ask for a list of satisfied customers. Talk to some of
  their previous clients and ask specifically whether
  their stands came in on time and within budget.
- Are they personable? Remember that you will be
  spending a fair amount of time with them, and it is
  essential that you find them both approachable and
  professional at all times.
- Where is their geographical location? Sometimes if
  the event is to be some way off from your present
  base, then distance could be a problem. But more
  importantly, try to choose companies that are within
  easy reach of your corporate location. Every time
  the designer comes to visit you it will cost, and if
  your project is complex there may well be numerous
  visits. Alternatively, if you decide to visit him, your
  time costs will start escalating.

- Finally, is your contractor a member of the *British Exhibition Contractors Association*? More than four in five such contractors in the UK are, and membership ensures a strict code of conduct and professionalism and good standards of workmanship.

Remember too that exhibition stands only have a very limited life expectancy and a good designer should be able to give the illusion of luxury without the stand being exorbitantly priced. Exhibition carpet, for instance, may look superb for the duration of a show, but would not stand up to continued wear and tear in the home environment over many years. (Having said that, exhibition carpet has to be able to stand very many pairs of shoes walking across it in a very limited time frame!)

At the outset it is imperative to give the designer an idea of the overall budget available. We will be returning to the question of budgeting tomorrow, but if your designer does not know the parameters under which you are expected to produce a show, then how can you expect him to deliver what you want? A good designer should be able to work within your budget and not exceed costs without your express approval beforehand.

We mentioned that an exhibition organiser will subcontract out many of the tasks in getting your stand the way you want it, but, of course, if you choose to organise the stand yourself you will need to brief these contractors yourself. In general you will need to think about getting contractors for:

- power
- lighting
- telephone lines
- carpets
- stand furniture
- plants and other decor
- security staff
- signage

Conferences and hospitality events are a little different!

We've been concentrating on exhibitions for the last few pages; but if you are planning on a conference, seminar, dinner or other type of meeting, then professional advice can be just as necessary. The way in which delegates react to the performances will not just be a question of how well rehearsed the presenters are, or whether the venue is ideal. If the design is not right it can have a very negative effect even before the first speaker has opened his mouth.

Staging a meeting is a theatrical event. You're trying, after all, to create an atmosphere in which your central message will be heard and accepted. So let's consider some of the elements of our performance.

The importance of theme
The design of the event needs to be co-ordinated throughout. That may seem self evident, but a central theme needs to run through from the very start so that the invitations and stationery reflect the same design as the signage, which in turn fit in with the decor thereby pulling everything together so that the branding is common throughout.

Lighting
Lighting is an area fraught with difficulty. If it is good, no-one notices it; if it is bad, the event can be ruined. Our advice is that if your budget is tight, the one area you should not skimp on is the lighting. It is simply no good thinking that if the audience can see what is happening, then all is well. If the set is mediocre and the venue is disappointing, the presence of a good lighting designer can often save the day, creating an environment that is vastly superior to what the basic set would have suggested.

Very often the lighting provided in hotels is unsuitable for larger events without extra being made available. Small meetings, however, may find the hotel lighting perfectly adequate, especially if such a venue is used for many such events. If you do need extra lighting, ensure that the hotel or conference centre can handle the extra power demands and that any lighting rigs can be supported by the building. Most professional organisers can tell you horror stories of conferences being plunged into darkness when the power demand from the extra lighting threw mains fuses.

Audio-visuals

At conferences and seminars, one of the main time consumers is getting the scripting and audio-visual material together and again the professional production company can play an invaluable role. So-called 'speaker support' in the way of slides, film and video are commonplace, and nowadays it has become the rule, rather than the exception, to use computer generated slides with packages such as Microsoft *PowerPoint*, Lotus *Freelance* and even HTML-generated pages displayed using an Internet browser.

The wide-scale adoption of computer generated slides reflects the ease with which many of these packages make simple and effective design available to all. Speakers generally prefer it if they can have total control over the production of their support material but the advent of computer generated displays gives the organiser an extra headache. In order to display computer slides you will need a projector which gives a bright enough picture to be seen in daylight by your audience and such projectors do not come cheap. For someone putting on only an occasional show it may be hard to justify spending around £4,000 for this equipment, together with the cost of bulb replacement and maintenance. The alternative is to hire such a projector and here the costs are in the region of £200 per day. Advertisements for these projectors can regularly be found in computer magazines and from computer peripheral stockists.

Conference producers
With so many aspects making up the overall stage-managed event, another specialist company worthy of consideration is the conference producer. Just as TV and radio programmes use producers to co-ordinate the overall look and feel and to pull together all the disparate elements that go into the making of the show, so too are producers a godsend to conference organisers.

The producer will organise the designer together with the sound and light technicians, the audio-visual effects, the stage build and, importantly, he will direct the show as it happens, cueing up speakers and performers, giving directions to the lighting crew, determining the correct timing for the audio-visual elements and being responsible for the autocue arrangements. If you want peace of mind, the conference producer is worth his weight in gold!

Administrative assistance

And if we are playing the rare metals game, the other 'must have' commodity for a successful conference is secretarial and administrative assistance. This is an area where in-house people can play a very positive role and make the life of an event organiser a great deal easier.

Before the event itself, delegates will be ringing up with a variety of questions and requests:

- does the catering include a vegetarian option?
- can you fax over a map – or can it be downloaded from the Web (frequently asked questions can be handled so effectively when the answers are posted on a Web site)?
- what transport is laid on?
- what of the accommodation available?

It will be impossible for you to be in all places at all times, so this basic support should be in the hands of someone you can rely upon, someone who is organised, proactive and personable. He will need to be computer-literate since so much organisation nowadays relies on the use of computer databases and word processing facilities. The administrative assistant will also be invaluable on the day itself (more of this on Friday) and the more you can hand across to him the better. Actually, although we have referred to 'him' throughout, would you think us terribly sexist if we were to say that the female temperament is ideally suited to this role, and in our experience some of the best administrators are women!

Finally, another reason for having a first rate assistant is that you will have more time mixing with the delegates on the day itself, giving you first hand reactions as to how the overall event is going.

Summary

So, today we have learned that although keeping within budget is of course necessarily important, some of the greatest contributors to success are the professional advisers and contractors available. Much as the lay person might be willing to try to organise everything, the path to a successful event is filled with booby traps into which the unwitting can fall all too easily.

So spread the load, use the professionals where they can add real value, and don't forget to find a first class administrative assistant!

Administrative essentials

Today we're going to concentrate on some of the essentials that many amateur organisers would much rather forget about, or at least put off until another day. Setting, and working within, a properly organised budget is all important, but equally important are the legal issues involved, not to mention the question of insurance.

Most legal issues stem in one form or another from the requirements of Health and Safety legislation. There are stringent rules and regulations which you ignore at your peril, for not only do a number of bodies ranging from the fire brigade to the local council have the right to close down your event with no warning, but if there is an accident arising from your negligence or ignorance, any subsequent court action could cost you dear. So always ask for advice – be it from the venue hosts, your stand contractors or any other experts you have to hand. At first glance it might feel as if they are trying to profit from you by insisting on supplying what you might consider to be optional extras; but it may well be that they are making these suggestions in order to fit in with legislation or local bye-laws. If in doubt, *ask*.

Budgets

It may seem obvious, but the ideal way to achieve a cost-effective exhibition or conference is to spend only what you need to and then no more. Like an addicted gambler, they have an uncanny propensity to absorb money like there is no tomorrow while showing little extra benefit for the extra spend.

From the very start you should have a clear idea of how much your event is going to cost. You should keep records of quotations, invoices, petty cash and any other movements of money within the overall equation and be able to calculate at any moment in time how close you are to budget. Make no mistake, the moment you start to let your budget take a back seat is the moment when your costs are liable to spiral out of control.

The first thing, then, is to make up a list of all your likely expenditure and potential income. It may be, for instance, that you will be able to attract sponsors or even sell tickets which you can offset against expenditure. Conferences and their ilk will of course have different budgeting priorities from exhibitions and other events. That is only natural. But there are many similarities as well, and of course there are also many events which combine a conference with an associated exhibition.

Remember that if you are likely to be staging regular events, a full and proper record of everything you have spent (and any incoming cash flow) will be invaluable the next time around. Could you have saved costs by doing this in such-and-such a way, or would additional expenditure in one area have solved a problem in another? It may seem boring at the time, but next time you organise a similar event you will be really pleased at having made the effort to keep proper records to which you can refer!

Too often in our experience someone who is new to staging events will inevitably ask the question 'How much can we afford?' Of course this is crucial; but we would suggest that a more sensible question would be 'How much do we have to spend in order to meet our objectives, and in what areas?'

It may seem labour intensive, and it is; but if you start by looking at your objectives and then drawing up a list of all the tasks necessary to achieve them – making an estimate of the costs involved – you will have a far stronger platform from which to begin. It will make you question the allocation of resources, as well as ensuring that you have given proper consideration to everything that is likely to be needed in staging the event in the first place.

Exhibiting costs

There is no hard and fast rule as to how much an exhibition will cost. Obviously the smaller regional and highly specialist exhibitions tend to be the cheapest because there will not be such a premium placed on space; but your biggest cost consideration is likely to be the type and size of your stand.

As we have already mentioned, there are basically two types of stand:

1. The shell-scheme, provided by the organiser.
2. The space-only stand for which you rent the space and provide the construction yourself.

The shell-scheme tends to work out as the cheaper option, albeit it may not look as exciting as a do-it-yourself build. Many inexperienced organisers tend to plump for the space-only option without a full appreciation of how much it will cost to fill the space. Normally you can expect the cost of the space itself to equate to around a quarter of the cost of the total stand. Up to a half of your budget could be spent on the stand design and construction.

IT'S ... DISTINCTIVE

Going for the shell-scheme option, you will be charged on a per-square-metre basis, so it is fairly easy to work out your overall commitment. Many exhibitions also offer packages which include the electrics, carpets, stand furniture, and so on, so it is well worth while talking to them to see what special deals they can offer you.

So our advice is that you should make a point of talking to a professional stand designer or contractor *before* you book any space so that there are no nasty surprises waiting to trip you up further down the line.

Here is a simple checklist of items that you will at least need to consider when costing your stand:

• overall space cost	• graphics
• shell scheme	• audio-visual equipment
• design	• handling and lifting costs
• construction	• transportation
• carpeting	• storage
• stand furniture	• fax hire
• telephone	• insurance
• electrics	• security
• water and waste	• cleaning
• flower displays	• catering

There will be other costs that you will need to consider, such as marketing your event, staffing costs and other peripherals. So make up similar lists for these.

Remember, too, that the larger the stand you have, the more people you will need to staff it; and this will have further implications on your overall budgeting. In general, travel, accommodation and subsistence can eat up a good quarter of your budget.

A final thought on exhibition stands: when it is not being used at an exhibition, could it be used for other purposes? Modular stands, especially, are often flexible enough to be adopted for all kinds of other functions such as travelling road shows, seminars and conferences, or even semi-permanent displays in your main office centre.

Conferences and hospitality

We have already seen that there will be many costs that have to be considered under both the headings of exhibitions and conferences. We have also noted that expenditure can be offset against potential income if you can get sponsorship for your event, or you can sell tickets for entry.

As a rough rule of thumb, delegates will be willing to pay for entry if some of the following conditions are met:

- they expect to learn something that could help them to improve their finances
- they expect to be able to update themselves on the latest issues
- they expect to be able to network with their peers
- they expect to be able to sell to other delegates
- they expect to enjoy an expenses-paid break from their normal work routine.

That last point may sound cynical, but go to any conference, seminar or hospitality event and we can all but guarantee that you will meet some who fall into that category!

So, if you are able to stage an accompanying exhibition with your conference or seminars, then there is a fair chance that you will be able to recoup a large proportion of your seminar costs, if not even make a profit on the whole venture. Of course, if it is an in-house event that you are organising, then you are unlikely to have that option, but never close your mind to any possibilities for raising money.

Alternatively you will have to ensure that your total costs can be met from any registration fees, subsidies from sponsors, commercial sponsorship and allowable company budget. So if you haven't done so already, get yourself a spreadsheet together into which you can enter costs and budgets and start working out a cash flow for the whole event. If you think you do not have the skills to experiment with 'what if' situations on your spreadsheet, then either make that a number one priority in your learning, or find someone who can do it for you. With the amount of computer software available nowadays, there really can be no excuse for you not to get to grips with this.

The main items on a conference budget are likely to be:

• hire of venue	• plants and other
• catering	decoration
• marketing	• signage
• printing and	• photography
documentation	• gifts and 'goodie bags'
• speakers' expenses	• gratuities to venue staff
• MC or toastmaster	• administration
expenses	• an extra for
• audio-visual equipment	contingencies – say 10%

The expenses set aside for speakers and for the chairman can be a major item in your budget. Equally, you might not have to pay a fee at all. It all depends on the arrangements and whether the speakers feel it to be in their interests to give their services for nothing. Either way, ensure you put in writing what agreements you have made. Not only will it display a professional approach, but you will also save the potential for embarrassment at a later date, especially if you have agreed to pay some speakers a fee whilst not paying others.

Equally important when working out your conference budget, try to split costs between those that are fixed – such as administration, venue hire, audio-visual and so on – and those that are variable – such as catering and out-of-hours functions.

If you are going to charge for attendance, you will need to strike a balance between the fee itself and the expected number of delegates. Charge too much and you will get fewer delegates; charge too little and you may have problems with your cash flow. Accurate budgeting therefore depends upon your ability to guess numbers at an early stage in the game, because once fixed and published, you will not be able to change your admission price.

Cash flow

The problem with organising any event is that your cash starts to flow out from your coffers at the very commencement of the planning process. Administration starts from day one, as will the costs for printing flyers and brochures and posting information on a Web site. Any way in which you can get cash flowing in at an early stage is therefore to be commended. Thus, it is no surprise that the majority of event organisers offer discounts for those who book early. You might even consider a sliding scale of discounts, so that the earlier the delegate books, the bigger the discount he gets.

At the same time, don't forget about the hidden extras. VAT is something that is all too easily overlooked, especially when getting quotations from contractors and other suppliers. Yet VAT normally has to be paid out before you are able to reclaim it, and this can have a substantial effect on your cash flow. Make sure you have a VAT entry line in your spreadsheet and then it will be more difficult to forget about.

Inflation is also something that you might have to consider if you are planning your event well enough in advance, for what you are quoted now may have increased somewhat by the time the event comes round. So, another rule of thumb: always check for how long a quoted price will remain valid.

Unforeseen expenses will always rear their ugly head, usually when you could least do with them. Your sales force might consider it necessary to order rounds of drinks in the bar and then to charge it to your budget. Telephone calls also have a magical way of expanding considerably when 'someone else' is paying.

So always allow enough for contingencies – say 10% of your overall budget, plus VAT of course!

Insurance

Whatever the size of your event, you can guarantee that old Murphy's Law will play a part in it – if there is anything that can possibly go wrong, it will. Insurance is therefore a vital consideration in your organising.

There are a number of areas where things can go badly
wrong:

- accidental injury to any of the participants
- accidental injury to the delegates
- unforeseen cancellation
- failure of speakers to show up at the time and place
  agreed
- loss or damage to personal property
- damage to the stand, shell-scheme, equipment or
  furniture
- theft of essential items

Basically, events insurance comes in two forms:

1. That which the organisers of an event insist upon.
2. That which you can take out for your own peace of
   mind.

Organisers of any public event will insist that you take out
Public Liability insurance and very often you will need to
provide proof that you have done so. This type of insurance
will cover you for any types of risk of personal injury or
damage to property caused by, or affecting, third parties,
including the period during the stand build and
breakdown.

It is obviously sensible to make sure that your stand,
including equipment and products, is insured for damage
and theft, and that your staff are covered for personal
injury and loss of personal belongings. This cover should
be not just for the event itself, but also whilst in transit to
and from the event. Because of the costs involved in

staging any kind of event it also pays to insure against unforeseen cancellation or postponement.

If you are organising an event somewhere abroad, further considerations become necessary. Health insurance – especially for countries such as the USA where hospital bills can be enormous – should come high up on your shopping list; and in some parts of the world you might even have to consider taking out insurance against kidnap and ransom. There are specialist brokers available who can quote for all types of cover.

Insurance should generally be placed at the time that the first contracts are being made, for losses and damage can occur at any time in the build up to the event, and the most 'dangerous' times are actually during the stand build and breakdown when accidents can happen because of someone hurrying to finish a job, and when theft or loss of goods is most likely to occur. (Insurance is great at concentrating the mind on considerations of security and we will be looking at this aspect on Friday.)

Finally, the question of insurance is not simply one of financial compensation. A great deal more than cash can be lost if things start to go wrong. So ensure, for instance, that key personnel travel to the venue separately, so that if there is an accident on the way at least some of them will get there. Don't put all your eggs in one basket – or to put it another way, where practicable ship your products or literature to the event in more than one car or van. Murphy's Law seems to outshine itself where the delivery of key props, literature and other essentials is concerned.

Summary

Today we have seen that budgeting is one of the most important aspects of organising any event since it will ensure that you:

- think of every aspect of putting on the event
- question the validity of every budget line
- give yourself a benchmark against which future events can be judged
- plan your cash flow.

We have also considered the importance both of complying with any legal requirements, and taking out insurance for when things go wrong.

Tomorrow we shall start to concern ourselves with getting people interested enough in our event to get them through the door.

Publicity and marketing

It doesn't matter how good an event you have arranged; if no one knows about it you are wasting your time. Pretty obvious? Well, you'd think so wouldn't you. Yet every year exhibitors and conference organisers across the country fail in this most basic task of an event manager to the extent that it sometimes seems simply a case of pot luck whether anyone bothers to attend an event or head for a specific item.

There are a multitude of ways of telling the world about your event. For example:

- national and regional press
- radio and TV
- trade and professional journals
- other forms of PR
- direct mail
- personal selling
- point of sale literature
- other exhibitions and events

Finding a medium shouldn't prove difficult – but care is needed with the message. To promote yourself effectively you should do your level best to match each of the event's objectives with your promotional strategy. For instance, if you are appearing at an exhibition, you are presumably doing so to meet a wider audience and introduce them to your products or services. Surely then it must be self evident that your promotional activities should concentrate on attracting visitors to your stand; and not just any visitors, but specifically those most likely to become your future customers – your prospects, rather than suspects.

So how do you do this? Well, there are basically two methods open to you. Either you can attract as many visitors to your stand as possible and, once they have come to your stand, try to sort the wheat from the chaff. Alternatively you identify your most likely prospects in advance and do everything in your promotional power to attract them to your promotion. Neither method is right or wrong; rather, it depends on your overall objectives in taking part in the first place.

And should your event happen to be an internal function don't think that justifies not worrying about attracting visitors, since they are a known quantity anyway. What about their expectations? Why are you inviting them in the first place? Wouldn't it help to get them into the right mind-set before they even set out for your chosen venue?

Before any major event you should try to co-ordinate your promotional activities carefully. After all, it is unlikely that your exhibition, conference, sales meeting, or whatever is an isolated event, so why treat it as such in your promotion? Promotion doesn't just begin and end before the event itself, either. Of course, pre-show promotion is important. It should generate more visitors than you would normally have got had you just sat back and waited to see who made the effort to come and see you. It should also generate press coverage which may influence some to pay you a visit, whilst others who cannot attend for whatever reason will still have been introduced to your products and services. But even during the show, especially at exhibitions, advertising, competitions and sponsorship can highlight your presence even in a large hall, and afterwards the resultant leads and mailing lists generated can be significant for your marketing efforts.

So let's look at some of the ways in which we can generate more interest in our event. First and foremost, your most useful ally has to be the press.

Public and media relations

It never fails to surprise us how some people treat journalists as an elite group who need to be pandered to obsequiously, and who regard it as some kind of honour to have been chosen for a write-up or interview, regardless of what finally ends up on the printed page or broadcast programme. If you think you might be in this camp of 'media toadies', then think again. Just who is doing whom the favour?

- Is he doing you a favour by giving you column inches or air time?
- Are you doing him a favour by providing him with material with which he can fill his air time or his column inches?

The answer, of course, is that one is dependent on the other. The journalist needs good stories. They are his life blood, and without them he cannot do a good job. You, on the other hand, need publicity, and what better way than coming to a mutually beneficial arrangement with the press? You might just be surprised at how easy it is to get your company or product featured.

Put yourself in the journalist's position. He firstly has to nose out the good stories before he can even begin to write them up. Now, if you were presented with piles of self-congratulatory notices how would you go about picking the best stories in the least possible time? Obviously you would go for the notices where the story was clearest, it gave the facts in the simplest way possible and where you did not have to wade through reams of superfluous product descriptions in order to see the wood for the trees.

So, follow these tips for guaranteed good press:

1. Write one press release for each product or service you wish to promote. If you insist on writing about all the products your company is involved with, you will only muddy the waters and make the journalist fight his way through trying to find the 'sexy option'.
2. If you are launching a new product or service, make sure this is clearly highlighted at the top of your

release. For instance '*Company ABC Launches New Product at Exhibition XYZ*'.

3. Allow plenty of white space on your press release. Don't be tempted to cram in as much as you can on to one side of paper. Not only is it intimidating on the eye, but it also makes it difficult for the journalist to jot down notes in the margins.

4. Try to encapsulate the main point of the story in the first paragraph and then expand the information in subsequent paragraphs. That way a journalist in a hurry will know at a glance if the story is worthy of his interest.

5. Give relevant figures to back up your story, especially product prices and the value of new contracts. This gives the resulting story more colour and depth and it saves the journalist having to ferret out the information himself.

6. Include colour photographs if they help the story along, but only if they are good enough for reproduction. Remember that a colour picture can be printed in mono, but the reverse is not true! Some journals have got into the habit of asking for companies to pay for colour separation charges, hoping they are desperate enough to do anything to get their story into print. In our view this is dishonest journalism – an attempt to stretch the magazine's advertising income – and we advise all our clients to refuse this moral blackmail. However, many do succumb; but we leave it to you to judge for yourself whether your story would have been covered anyway.

7. Don't forget to include a contact name, phone number, fax and e-mail address so that the journalist can come back for more information. Indeed, we often find that if you arouse a journalist's curiosity enough you can almost guarantee a plethora of phone calls over the next 24 hours. Our favourite was a single paragraph that reported that company A had just signed an £8m contract with company B. No further details. Just the contact numbers for more information. The trade journals who had heard of company B wanted to know all about company A. The regional press wanted to learn about the local angle. And the national press wanted the full story!

8. Finally, send in your story in plenty of time. It is simply no good sending something in two days before the event and hoping that it will get space. Do you really think the journalist is going to leave all his writing until the last minute in case he gets any hot news?

If you have a stand at someone else's event, then find out if they have a press office or PR representative and if they do, then keep them fully informed of any product launches or other news you might have. Again, both sides benefit from this kind of arrangement. And you might even find there is an official show preview that is mailed to potential visitors to raise their interest. If you can get a story about your company into one of these publications, then the chances are that you will get more interest in your part of the show come the actual event itself.

Perhaps the most important piece of advice regarding public relations we can give is that you should concentrate on selling the benefits of your product or service, not on its features. Most people buy for reasons of fear or greed. If a customer is considering buying a product or service (and an event – be it a seminar, conference or exhibition – is a service) he is not necessarily interested in the physical attributes of the product, but in what benefits will accrue to him if he does make the purchase.

If you are at all unsure how to put this into practice, try a simple exercise. In any of your publicity blurb, try adding the phrase 'which means that' or perhaps 'so that' in order to link a feature with the benefits it brings. You could end your copy with a one liner such as 'Following this event, delegates will be able to……' and list a few positive key factors to which the delegate can relate.

Getting the press along to an exhibition is a great deal easier than to a conference or seminar. Unless the latter are likely to be controversial, there needs to be a very good reason for the media to put aside a morning, or even a whole day on the basis that they might be lucky to get a story at all. If the media is invited, then make sure that there is someone who is delegated to look after them and help them get all the information they need. Remember, without being taken for a ride, if you help them out, they are more likely to help you out.

Direct mail

We noted that there are plenty of other ways of getting people interested in your event and one of the most successful has to be direct mail. This, of course, is dependent on the message you are trying to put across and the quality of the mailing list employed.

One of the most effective ways of getting people to your event is to mail complimentary tickets to them. On average around half the people attending trade events do so on a complimentary basis; for computer exhibitions that number increases dramatically.

If you are one of many with a stand at that particular show, then give good reasons in an accompanying letter why your prospective visitor should make the effort to visit your stand. He may well have got invitations from some of your competitors and so this is no game for retiring wall-flowers. Be specific about new products and services that you will be demonstrating so they have a good reason to visit you. You could perhaps even offer some kind of incentive (we'll consider a few shortly).

Apart from mailing to prospective clients on your own in-house databases, you will want to attract new prospects, so consider turning to list brokers, publishers or exhibition managers. List brokers tend to be able to offer a variety of lists from varying sources, but the owners of the lists still have power of veto as to what is sent out. You cannot actually buy the list outright; all you can do is to rent it for the occasion in question. Typically such a list might cost around £100 per 1,000 names and it will normally be supplied as a strip of self-adhesive address labels. Some list owners refuse even to let you have the labels, and you therefore have to give your mailings to them to post. If you are not VAT-registered, do make sure that you pre-pay the postage, otherwise you are liable to pay this tax if it is charged to you retrospectively.

When selecting lists, do remember that those you can obtain from trade magazines differ in their usefulness, depending on whether they are subscription lists or controlled circulation. Because controlled circulation magazines normally make their money from advertising, they are generally free of charge to their readers. In order to receive the publication the reader is normally asked for personal information which provides the basis of the lists. So this type of list tends to be comprehensive and you can sometimes sort by quite detailed criteria.

Lists obtained from exhibition organisers can be extremely detailed since, if they have done half a reasonable job, they can ask visiting delegates quite a number of key questions about their respective companies and interests. It is quite normal, for instance, for such lists to have details of:

- the main company activity
- where it is located
- company size
- your job title
- which type of products interest you
- purchasing authority
- when you are likely to consider your next purchase
- your available budget.

By cross-correlating your search criteria, you can therefore be quite specific as to which prospects you wish to mail-shot.

Advertising

It is very difficult to analyse precisely the value gained from advertising. Nevertheless, it is pretty clear that the more your company's name and products are seen by prospective clients before, during and after an event, the more it will register with them.

Advertising for and at an event need not necessarily be expensive, as long as it is incorporated into your planned advertising campaign. If you were going to be advertising in a trade magazine already, for instance, then it might be a good idea to insert a one-liner inviting visitors to such-and-such an event to come to your stand.

If your budget will allow, it might be worth inserting an advert into a specific trade magazine which is likely to be read by visitors to the show. Most magazines offer full page, half page and quarter page advertising rates – more for a colour ad – and sometimes you can be quite specific as to where it will be placed. Remember too that the closer the magazine is to its printing date, the more power you have in your negotiation to get that advertising rep to lower his rates. It would be a foolish advertising manager who turned down the prospect of a lower advertising rate in favour of no advertising income from you at all; unless, of course, he had already sold his allocation of ad spaces for that edition. So you will need to play your cards carefully in this regard, juggling cost against being left with the worst ad positioning in the mag.

Advertising in the show catalogue is also considered highly effective, not only because visitors will be constantly reminded of your company name as they wander round the event, but also because many visitors will keep their catalogue as a source of reference long after the show is over.

Sponsorship

One of the fastest growing areas of promotional activity, especially at exhibitions, is that of sponsorship. Virtually anything can be sponsored these days, but if you bear in mind the desire for your name to be at the forefront of people's recollection as they wander around the event, then sponsoring

- carrier bags
- restaurant serviettes
- risers on stairways
- posters and banners
- product locator boards

and so on make perfect sense. You might even be able to sponsor courtesy coaches taking visitors to the centre. Just because the event manager has not offered a sponsorship facility does not mean that you shouldn't ask if you feel it would be right for featuring your company or product.

Incentives

Everyone likes a bargain; even better, we all like something for nothing, and incentivising delegates is a first class way of getting people to your stand or to the event itself.

Incentives come in all shapes and sizes, be they give-aways and competitions, or special price reductions on goods being sold. Above all, though, they should be imaginative and they should be relevant to the message you are trying to promote.

We remember once going to a computer show in Olympia where a firm succeeded in drawing in the majority of visitors passing its stand by offering a very simple competition to win a cuddly toy. So much effort was spent in promoting the ease of winning (we came away with not one, but three furry tiger cubs!) that no one on the stand thought to link them in any way either with the firm itself or with what they were selling. To this day we cannot recall either the name of the firm or why it had bothered turning up to the show (but the little tigers make a good talking point beaming down from one of the book shelves in the office).

Remember to let everyone know about your incentive. That means telling the show organisers and the trade press, making sure it is mentioned in the show catalogue, advising the Master of Ceremonies or toastmaster or printing it in the programme. Give-aways can also be a great idea to send out with your invitations.

There are very many firms that specialise in supplying promotional gifts and, not surprisingly, they come much cheaper if bought in bulk. So remember to include such a strategy as part of your overall marketing effort. Allow a lead time of perhaps three months for the necessary printing to be applied to the gifts; that way you will not end up with a shoddy, hurried job.

Finally, competitions can be good, not only in attracting visitors to your stand, but also in creating a database to which you can send mail-outs in the future. Many event organisers invite delegates to drop their visiting cards in a bowl to win a prize on the first-out-of-the-hat principle. Of course, that may be fine if you just want to get loads of unqualified leads; wouldn't it be better if you could qualify them in some little way at least – such as by asking one or two simple questions? That way you might also be able to carry out some market research on your product range or company image, for instance.

Summary

Today we have seen that the success of an event is often in no small measure down to the amount of effort expended on its promotion. Effective public relations relies on establishing a rapport with the media, and if you treat them well, helping them to do a good job, you will reap the dividends in terms of press coverage and editorial.

Promotion can be further enhanced by the use of direct mail, advertising, sponsorship and incentives, but at all times the central message that you are attempting to put across must take precedence over everything else.

Tomorrow, to quote a well-worn saying, is the end of the beginning and the beginning of the end. So have an early night and we look forward to seeing you first thing in the morning.

Almost there!

After what could be months of careful planning we're poised at the culmination of the event itself. There are a few last minute arrangements to be made, though, so let's go through our checklist to ensure that nothing has been forgotten.

Exhibitions and trade fairs enjoy a very different pre-show timescale from conferences, seminars, awards and gala dinners. So let's start by considering the pre-exhibition build-up.

Stand builders may need up to three or four contractors to prepare a stand, depending on its complexity. However, for smaller exhibitions – especially those held in hotels – it is more usual to be allocated part of the previous day, continuing through the night if necessary. It is here that shell-scheme stands really come in to their own. Either way, though, you have to allow enough time to dress the stand once the initial build has been completed.

In large exhibition halls, electricians, plumbers, carpet layers and many others will be following a highly planned operation and it is usually best to leave them well alone rather than get in the way at this early stage. Stand fitters are always under pressure from time and they do not appreciate being held up by what they regard as unnecessary questions. As they are working to specific instructions, they will not make any changes without instruction from their site representative anyway, so if you have to raise a question, discuss it with the designer or representative only.

Before the opening of the exhibition itself, the entire venue has to be inspected by fire and health and safety inspectors, and all of their requirements should have been explicitly laid out in the rules and regulations given by the show organisers.

Security is a particular worry, especially during the final stages of stand dressing. You can guarantee that the parking bay which you have been allocated will be what seems miles from your stand itself, and because of the security risk, not least from your competitors, you should always have someone on the stand, particularly in the lunch break when many thefts can occur. Most exhibitions usually provide some sort of security on the 'get-in' day and at night, but you should still make a point of locking anything away that can possibly 'walk off on its own'.

Staffing the stand

It's time for another self evident statement! Regardless of how superb your stand is, how innovative your products are, or how enticing your advertising and incentives, if your stand staff are either ill-mannered or ill-informed they can literally negate everything you have striven to achieve over all these months.

The environment of an exhibition is very different from the normal sales setting, and surprisingly there are very many people who do not seem to realise this. When selecting stand personnel it is essential to pick personable people who can engage visitors and identify sales prospects quickly and easily; they need to be highly familiar with the company's products and they must also get on with one another!

When looking for your stand staff, remember the following criteria that they should all possess:

- self confidence, to engage total strangers in conversation
- personality, to put visitors at ease
- communications skills, to help get the message across
- negotiating skills, to help them glean information to help place an order
- in-depth knowledge of the company's products or services.

The number of staff you will need will naturally depend on stand size and for how long the show runs. Exhibitions are demanding environments in which to work; your feet quickly tire, your voice starts to croak, you might desperately need to go to the loo, and if the stand manager has not properly thought out the staffing levels you can quickly end up with dispirited staff. Not the best environment in which to try to sell anything! So make up a duty roster and ensure that your staff stick to it, enforcing breaks in which they can get a change of atmosphere and relax.

Staffing an exhibition stand is not, however, just about fielding sales staff. Very often you will need to consider a whole range of other skills as well:

- technical staff
- demonstration staff
- financial and credit control staff
- senior managers and/or directors
- administrative staff.

Make sure that everyone knows his role well before the start of the exhibition, preferably at least the night before the opening.

There are plenty of dos and don'ts when staffing a stand, many more than we can possibly cover here, but it is important that staff should understand the effect their behaviour has on others. How many times, for instance, have you been to exhibitions where the staff 'stand guard' on the edge of the stand almost daring you to enter?

Equally off-putting are those who converse amongst themselves, all but ignoring any visitor, or those who look bored – if you are not interested in your company's products can you really expect anyone else to be?

Exhibition stands quickly become untidy places given half a chance, and so it is vital to look out for anything that might let the stand down, especially later in the day. It goes without saying that dirty cups and plates should be cleared when the visitor departs; but stand tidiness also includes a ready supply of literature, and an absence of stand staff filling time during their scheduled breaks.

Visitor details

Capturing the details of your stand visitors is essential at an exhibition since your sales team will want to make contact with potential purchasers later on. Collecting business cards is not a very efficient method of doing this since you rarely have enough room to write down on the back any relevant details which have come up during that visit. Enquiry pads might be adequate for small exhibitions or for those with a limited amount of products on show. However, if you or your sales team design your own form you can help ensure that your stand staff don't forget important information which it is all too easy to do in the excitement of the show.

At larger exhibitions, it is normal for the organiser to offer exhibitors electronic lead recording whereby a light-pen can read bar codes attached to visitors' badges. Some allow such pen-readers to be attached to a computer database, recording many details and allowing fast turnaround for post-event follow-up.

Here is a list of the kind of questions your staff might do well to ask:

- Name, position, company, address and phone number (you might find it easier simply to staple the visitor's business card to your form)
- The size and business of his company
- Products and services of specific interest
- Products and suppliers/manufacturers currently used
- Budget available and purchasing authority
- Recommended follow-up – send further literature? arrange a demo? prepare a written quotation?
- Additional comments.

Finally, don't forget that bag of essentials that all stand managers should possess. Because most of us take for granted all the little everyday essentials that we can simply reach out for in the office, it comes as a bitter blow to find we have left behind:

- sticky 'Post-it' notes
- paper clips
- highlighter pens
- sticky tape
- a good supply of pens and pencils
- visiting cards
- safety pins
- mirror
- first aid kit
- a telephone contacts book.

Pre-conference check

Conferences, seminars and other meetings have a different set of requirements prior to the opening and here a good degree of organisation pays dividends in terms of saved frustration.

You cannot over-check that everything is as it should be, and a properly laid out checklist will help you ensure that nothing is missed. It never does any harm to put in a quick call to the venue a few days beforehand to check that they still know about the conference. Double bookings do occur, although if you have put everything in order, it will be up to the venue to sort out their own mistakes. A telephone call to the suppliers of any equipment is also a useful memory jogger.

Unlike with an exhibition, it can be quite a good idea for the conference manager to arrive before stand or set build to ensure that the room is in the condition expected and that access for any equipment is available. Check for any damage prior to your equipment arriving as you certainly do not want to be held responsible for the negligence of others.

One of your first jobs will be to establish an organiser's office where anyone – be he delegate or team member – can go to, or telephone, for advice. It should be permanently staffed so that any messages can be just about guaranteed to reach their intended recipients.

Go through with the venue manager the details of everything for which they will be responsible. Coffee and tea breaks should be agreed with firm times so that both sides know what is expected to happen and when.

Rehearsals

If your conference is to be a success, then rehearsals are an absolute necessity. Don't allow anyone involved with the show to skip the main rehearsals – certainly not the final rehearsal. And that goes for the Managing Director or Chief Executive, just as much as the other participants.

Sometimes technical rehearsals are necessary before the full rehearsals, depending on the complexity of the show. For these it is normally better for the speakers not to be present since the technicians will be concentrating on other aspects of the show and so their priorities will appear so different that it might suggest to the participants that chaos is all around them!

Before any speaker rehearsals, check that people are happy with their script. There is simply no point in going through with it if they are not. If an autocue is being used, then a properly finished script is essential at least a couple of days before the event. Check that the lighting is adequate for the speaker to be able to read his notes and, importantly, that the lectern is neither too high, nor too low for him. A wrongly positioned lectern can ruin a speaker's confidence and do irreparable damage to his performance.

For the final rehearsal, try to make it as realistic as possible. Someone should be positioned at the door with instructions to admit no one, and a small audience of friends and colleagues should be assembled together to give positive criticism. Time each element of the show, in case adjustments need to be made at the last minute. If you know that one section has over-run, then you can warn the venue staff that coffee or tea might have to be delayed by 20 minutes. They may not be happy at the delay, but at least they won't be left killing time until your delegates arrive to find the coffee is cold.

Registration

For most delegates, the registration area will be the first impression they get of the conference itself and one of the best ways of getting such an event off to a good start is to organise a smooth and trouble-free registration process.

In general terms, if delegates have pre-registered, then one member of your staff should be able to hand them their badges and any delegate packs at the rate of about 100 every hour. On-site registration, however, will reduce this to about 20 an hour. It is usually better to ensure that there are too many registration staff than too few. Try to ensure there is some kind of continuity between their uniforms and the colour scheme of the event itself.

Badges are a lot easier to handle if, together with meal vouchers, personal timetables and anything else which changes from delegate to delegate, they are placed in well-marked envelopes which are alphabetically filed. Badges laid out on tables tend to generate a free-for-all atmosphere and should be avoided for all but the smallest meetings.

Attendance lists are usually welcomed by delegates because of the help it gives them in networking. Arrange the names either in alphabetical order, or by company name, but ensure that everyone gets a copy.

If there is a to be a formal sit-down dinner, then giving the delegates prior information about which tables they are sitting at can help in the smooth running of the event; but be aware that there will always be some awkward customers who will want to change where they are sitting and will expect the organiser to put it at the top of his priority list!

Assuming the worst

It doesn't matter how much you have prepared and how many rehearsals you have gone through; when it comes to crunch time Mr Murphy will do his level best to ensure his law will not be broken. If anything can go wrong, now is the time that it will happen. Perhaps your guest speaker has taken it upon himself to take the train to Newcastle-upon-Tyne whereas your event is all ready to roll in Newcastle-under-Lyme. Your A-V projector might blow its bulb, the set might fall apart or the air conditioning might break down.

Managing events is not something for the seriously paranoid, and if you start to worry about all the possible mishaps that could befall your special show, you could end up a gibbering wreck.

But worrying unduly is not the same as making plans of what you would do should things go wrong. It is well said that the mark of a true professional event organiser is the ability to think ahead, troubleshoot and come up with a fix.

A-V projector bulbs regularly fail, so an experienced organiser will have ensured that a member of the technical staff is not only delegated to be responsible for changing the bulb at short notice, but that he can even do so in the dark. Better still, that there is enough light for him to see what he is doing!

The failure of a speaker to turn up? Because you will have the timings from the full rehearsal, you will be in a better position to juggle around the order of the event at the last minute to keep the show moving.

The way in which you react in times of calamity is also very important. If you remain cool, calm and collected, you will have a pacifying effect on others and you will be better able to make rational decisions. If others see you as being totally in control it will improve the chances of the event not turning into a flop before your very eyes. At the very least, therefore, try to think through in advance as many adverse possibilities as you can and plan what you would do should any of them occur.

Summary

Today we have seen that the care and attention given to small details will play a significant part in the success of an event. The success of exhibitions relies to a great extent on the calibre of the staff you employ and tracking visitor details needs to be well thought out.

Conferences need a great deal of last minute preparation, but again, pre-planning the details will allow you to concentrate on the main picture, from when the rehearsals get under way to the moment the show kicks off.

It's been a long time in the planning, but finally we've got our show on the road.

Clear up, wash up and post mortem

The show's over and the crowds are finally leaving, but for the show organiser the work is far from done. For a start there is the dismantling of the stand and clearance of the venue.

Whether it has been an exhibition or a conference, the main priority is to get clear of the venue, and for this strict discipline is essential. So much *can* go wrong at this point in time, that it should be an integral part of your overall planning.

First things first, and you should ensure that all the small, easily portable items are put away first. All equipment must be thoroughly checked, and those who have planned for this by storing the boxes in which it all came in a logical sequence will save themselves hours of trouble later.

It is sometimes surprising to behold how many of your loyal stand staff – who may well have done an excellent job throughout the whole show – will suddenly remember that they have an urgent appointment to get to and depart with the main rush of people assuming there will always be someone to clear up after them. Avoid this at all costs by allocating people's roles and responsibilities beforehand. Thefts at show breakdowns are also very common and only by ensuring that everything is accountable and that someone is responsible for each piece of equipment will you guarantee not to be one of the victims.

The breakdown of an exhibition moves very quickly normally, and all the sites need to be checked for damage as they are cleared. It is usually a requirement for the exhibitors to leave their stand space absolutely clear – and this includes removing each scrap of sticky tape on the floor. As this is a time-consuming process it tends to get left to 'someone else' to do, but the exhibitor will end up being charged if the venue has to arrange such a clear up.

It is not uncommon for some venues that have a minimal refurbishment budget to try to get conference and exhibition organisers to pay for normal wear and tear on the building, in which case pre- and post-site inspections in the company of one of the venue officials would be absolutely essential.

Settling up

It seems to take many people by surprise when many of the bills come in ages after the exhibition or conference is finished. In the heat of the moment it is easy to agree something that will have to be paid for sooner or later, and months later it can be very difficult to remember exactly how much something was supposed to have cost – unless you have stuck rigidly to your system of recording every expense as and when it was agreed. There really is no substitute for a proper budgetary control.

Accounting for food and drink is often one of the most difficult aspects of budget control, but if the organiser had the forethought to insist to the venue that any agreed over-run must be signed off by one named person only, then you will be in a much stronger position if the venue subsequently comes back to you with a long list of extras provided on request.

Following up leads

Following a successful exhibition you should have gathered a large amount of sales leads and after any other type of event there will undoubtedly be at least two or three contacts you want to get in touch with. Yet at the very time when they should be able to reap the benefits of having staged the event at all, far too many companies change down to a lower gear and turn their mind to other important things. Excuses vary, but usually include variations on the following:

- *Lack of time* – there is always a full in-tray awaiting you on your return and it is all too easy to find excuses for putting off the follow up.
- *Lack of resources* – for some companies the number of leads acquired seems to come as a surprise; a lack of qualification of leads during the event itself only compounds the problem.
- *Lack of trust in the leads* – usually as a direct result of the failure by stand staff to qualify the leads.
- *Assuming that your leads will call you* – and who do

you think you are kidding? Meanwhile your
competitors are chasing them up and leaving you
way behind at the back of the queue!

Yet it tends to be the case that leads gleaned from
exhibitions are more likely to be converted into actual sales
than from most other avenues. (The best leads, of course,
are referrals from existing customers!) The point is to
ensure that they are followed up quickly and tracked
accurately. So the event does not stop when you strike the
set and go home. It stops when you have followed up the
leads, paid the bills, and had the post mortem (of which
more later).

Researching the event

In all the euphoria at the end of the conference or seminar
the one question that is often not asked is 'was it all worth
it?'. And perhaps that is right, for the time when *not* to ask
any such question is whilst everyone is still on a high.

Far better to ask the question, though, a week or two after
the event once everyone has had a chance to get back into
the normal swing of things and to consider if any of the
messages of the conference have actually been
remembered. Try to put together a questionnaire which
reflects some of the aims of the conference in the first place
to see if these have been met. It might even be worthwhile
asking what the delegates thought of the venue, of the
catering, the transport and other points relating to
infrastructure.

There is always a danger that some of the delegates will

put down what they think the organiser wants to hear, so it should be explained that only honest answers will help ensure a better event next time around. Many large companies undertake research into the effectiveness of their advertising, and the same care should be taken in getting good feedback after an event.

Post-exhibition

Feedback after an exhibition is just as important. Naturally you will not be able to poll the visitors, but there will be many of the exhibition team who have opinions that are worth canvassing and which will give you a good grounding for future events.

In trying to decide if the event really has been worth it, a good place to start is to work out if it succeeded in fulfilling the aims and objectives set for it. So let's go back to our original lists and compare notes…

The criteria for evaluating success will be many and varied, but are likely to include some of the following:

- Were the objectives achieved in full or in part?
- Did the delegates leave feeling satisfied with the event?
- Was the venue suitable?
- Did the event end up within budget?
- Was enough lead time allowed for effective participation?
- Were any deadlines missed? If so, can you ascertain why?
- Was the administration effective and efficient?
- Was the core message adequately put across to the audience?

Just as important as knowing what went right is what went wrong – and why? Knowing the answers to that will ensure that mistakes are not repeated next time. And knowing what aspects were the most successful will help you plan an even more successful event next time. It's a good idea to keep the considered responses to these questions in a file so that when the next event comes around you will have a good source of reference to refer to. Not only will it give you a head start next time around, but when it is time for you to move on, your successor won't be starting off from scratch.

There is one other very important reason for you to document everything; and that is that when all the shouting is over you will be able to provide documented evidence on just how rewarding the show has been to those that hold the purse strings! In fact we would go further and urge you to ensure that a copy of the final report is given to the directors, spelling out the highs and the lows with some quotes from the respondents to bring it alive.

The staff also need to know how they performed. Platitudes are not, in the long run, really appreciated and many will appreciate being told if there was anything they could have done better. But keep it confidential. No one will thank you for highlighting their deficiencies for all to see! The technical crews should not be forgotten either, for their contributions can make or break a show.

Epilogue

Throughout this week we have been preaching one central theme that we hope has been communicated effectively.

For a successful event, be it an exhibition, seminar, conference or other type of show, nothing can substitute for effective planning, along with some flexibility, lateral thinking and good-humoured resilience.

A successful event can be measured in many ways, but by clearly delegating, letting everyone know what part they play in the overall scheme of things, and by keeping a beady eye on the budgets, you are ensuring the basic foundations from which a successful event can come alive.

Further *Successful Business in a Week* **titles from Hodder & Stoughton and the Institute of Management all at £6.99**

All Hodder & Stoughton books are available from your local bookshop or can be ordered direct from the publisher. Just tick the titles you want and fill in the form below. Prices and availability subject to change without notice.

To: Hodder & Stoughton Ltd, Cash Sales Department, Bookpoint, 39 Milton Park, Abingdon, Oxon, OX14 4TD. If you have a credit card you may order by telephone – 01235 400414.
E-mail address: orders@bookpoint.co.uk

Please enclose a cheque or postal order made payable to Bookpoint Ltd to the value of the cover price and allow the following for postage and packaging:
UK & BFPO: £4.30 for one book; £6.30 for two books; £8.30 for three books.
OVERSEAS & EIRE: £4.80 for one book; £7.10 for 2 or 3 books (surface mail).

Name: ....

Address: ....

....

If you would prefer to pay by credit card, please complete:

Please debit my Visa/Mastercard/Diner's Card/American Express (delete as appropriate) card no:

❏ ❏ ❏ ❏ ❏ ❏ ❏ ❏ ❏ ❏ ❏ ❏ ❏ ❏ ❏ ❏

Signature .... Expiry Date ....

Business Checklists titles from Hodder & Stoughton and the Institute of Management all at £8.99

0 340 74292 5	Information & Financial Management	❐
0 340 74290 9	Marketing & Strategy	❐
0 340 74291 7	Operations & Quality Management	❐
0 340 74288 7	People Management	❐
0 340 74294 1	Personal Effectiveness & Career Development	❐
0 340 74289 5	Personnel Policies, Training & Development	❐
0 340 74293 3	Small Business Management	❐

All Hodder & Stoughton books are available from your local bookshop or can be ordered direct from the publisher. Just tick the titles you want and fill in the form below. Prices and availability subject to change without notice.

To: Hodder & Stoughton Ltd, Cash Sales Department, Bookpoint, 78 Milton Park, Abingdon, Oxon, OX14 4TD. If you have a credit card you may order by telephone – 01235 400414
fax – 01235 400454
E-mail address: orders@bookpoint.co.uk

Please enclose a cheque or postal order made payable to Bookpoint Ltd to the value of the cover price and allow the following for postage and packaging:

UK & BFPO: £4.30 for one book; £6.30 for two books; £8.30 for three books.

OVERSEAS & EIRE: £4.80 for one book; £7.10 for 2 or 3 books (surface mail).

Name: ....

Address: ....

....

If you would prefer to pay by credit card, please complete:
Please debit my Visa/Mastercard/Diner's Card/American Express (delete as appropriate) card no:

☐ ☐ ☐ ☐ ☐ ☐ ☐ ☐ ☐ ☐ ☐ ☐ ☐ ☐ ☐ ☐ ☐ ☐

Signature .... Expiry Date ....